WG

The Guide to
Better Birthdays

The Guide to
Better Birthdays

A Celebration of Great Ideas
About the Beauty of Life and
The Passage of Time

Compiled and Edited by Criswell Freeman

WALNUT GROVE PRESS
Nashville, TN 37205

ISBN 1-887655-35-2

The ideas expressed in this book are not, in all cases, exact quotations, as some have been edited for clarity and brevity. In all cases, the author has attempted to maintain the speaker's original intent. In some cases, material for this book was obtained from secondary sources, primarily print media. While every effort was made to ensure the accuracy of these sources, the accuracy cannot be guaranteed. For additions, deletions, corrections or clarifications in future editions of this text, please write WALNUT GROVE PRESS.

Printed in the United States of America
Cover Design by Mary Mazer
Typesetting & Page Layout by Sue Gerdes
Editor for Walnut Grove Press: Alan Ross
3 4 5 6 7 8 9 10 •   99 00 01

ACKNOWLEDGMENTS
The author gratefully acknowledges the helpful support of Angela Beasley, Dick and Mary Freeman, and Mary Susan Freeman.

For My Grandmother, Marie T. Freeman

On Her 100th Birthday

Table of Contents

A Message to Readers

Because you're reading a book with the word "birthday" in its title, you're probably celebrating another year of life. Congratulations! Birthdays are tailor-made for celebration so, above all, enjoy yourself. But amid the good times, you may also wish to consider the implications of having lived another year on the planet. If so, this book is designed to help.

On the pages that follow, some of history's greatest thinkers ask you to examine your life, where you've been, and where you are going. Each chapter consists of a collection of related quotations; taken together, the quotes are intended as a catalyst for constructive thinking and planning. As you read these pages, you may choose to sharpen your focus or redirect your efforts. If you do so, you will have given yourself a priceless birthday gift.

Robert Louis Stevenson observed, "There is no duty so much underrated as the duty of being happy." Do your duty and have a happy birthday. And while you're at it, celebrate a life that is like no other: yours.

1

It's Your Birthday: Enjoy It

Elbert Hubbard advised, "Happiness is a habit. Cultivate it." This advice is always in season, but particularly so on birthdays. So count your blessings, give yourself a pat on the back, treat yourself to something special, and practice the happiness habit.

Contentment is a gift we give ourselves. It follows that a happy birthday starts on the inside and works its way out. If you're searching for a better birthday, or any other day for that matter, remember that happiness — one of life's most beautiful flowers — is always cultivated between the ears.

One cannot have
too large a party.

Jane Austen

Man only plays when, in the full meaning
of the word, he is a man. And he is only
completely a man when he plays.

Schiller

People miss their share of happiness,
not because they never found it, but because
they didn't stop to enjoy it.

William Feather

Happiness is a matter of your own doing.
You can be happy or you can be unhappy.
It's just according to the way
you look at things.

Walt Disney

The clearest sign of wisdom
is continued cheerfulness.

Michel de Montaigne

Brief is the space of life allotted to you;
    pass it as pleasantly as you can,
    not grieving from noon till eve.

Euripides

My crown is called content,
    a crown that seldom kings enjoy.

William Shakespeare

Think contentment the greatest wealth.

George Shelley

Life is a journey, not a destination; and
    happiness is not "there" but here;
    not tomorrow, but today.

Sidney Greenberg

Most people are about as happy
    as they make up their minds to be.

Abraham Lincoln

Happiness is a habit.
Cultivate it.

Elbert Hubbard

The longer we dwell
on our misfortunes,
the greater is their
power to harm us.

Voltaire

Finish every day and be done with it.
You have done what you could;
some blunders and absurdities have crept in;
forget them as soon as you can.

Ralph Waldo Emerson

The growth of wisdom may be gauged
accurately by the decline of ill-temper.

Nietzsche

We are all crazy when we are angry.

Philemon

Anger tortures itself.

Publilius Syrus

An inexhaustible good nature is one
of the most precious gifts of heaven.

Washington Irving

He who sings frightens away his ills.

Miguel de Cervantes

Music is a higher revelation
than philosophy.

Ludwig van Beethoven

Happiness doesn't depend upon
who you are or what you have; it depends
upon what you think.

Dale Carnegie

Happiness is not a state to arrive at, but a manner of traveling.

Samuel Johnson

G enius is childhood recaptured.

Charles Baudelaire

E very child is an artist. The problem is how
to remain an artist once he grows up.

Pablo Picasso

M iddle age is when you don't have
to have fun to enjoy yourself.

Franklin P. Jones

C herish all your happy moments.
They make a fine cushion for old age.

Christopher Morley

Wrinkles should merely indicate where smiles have been.

Mark Twain

There is only one way to happiness,
and that is to cease worrying about things
that are beyond the power of our will.

Epictetus

To live happily is an inward power
of the soul.

Marcus Aurelius

The happiness of your life depends
upon the quality of your thoughts;
therefore guard accordingly.

Marcus Aurelius

Happiness and misery depend as much
on temperament as on fortune.

La Rochefoucauld

Nothing is good or bad but
thinking makes it so.

William Shakespeare

Do not let trifles disturb your tranquillity
of mind. Life is too precious to be sacrificed
for the nonessential and transient. Ignore the
inconsequential.

Grenville Kleiser

Contentment is a perishable commodity.
That's what makes it so precious.

Burgess Meredith

Laugh and the world laughs with you.
Weep and you weep alone.

Ella Wheeler Wilcox

Happiness means having something to do
and something to live for.

Bishop Fulton J. Sheen

Is not life a hundred times too short for us
to bore ourselves?

Nietzsche

Whatever you do, do it
with all your heart and soul.

Bernard Baruch

To love what you do and feel that it matters —
how could anything else be more fun?

Katharine Graham

This is the true joy in life, the being used
for a purpose recognized by yourself
as a mighty one.

George Bernard Shaw

Life is not breath, but action.
Life consists less in length of days than in the
keen sense of living.

Jean-Jacques Rousseau

When a man is willing and eager,
the gods join in.

Aeschylus

A sad soul can kill you quicker than a germ.

John Steinbeck

Be. Live. And don't worry too much
about the troubles that loom so large today.
They will pass.

Mickey Rooney

The present will not long endure.

Pindar

Do not borrow trouble by dreading
tomorrow. It is the dark menace of the future
that makes cowards of us all.

Dorothy Dix

While the fates permit, live happily.
Life speeds on with hurried step,
and with winged days the wheel
of the headlong year is turned.

Seneca

I am an optimist. It does not seem
too much use being anything else.

Winston Churchill

Life has so much fun in it. Look for
the comic relief, and you can't be unhappy
for long.

Carl Reiner

No longer forward nor behind
I look in hope or fear;
But, grateful, take the good I find,
The best of now and here.

John Greenleaf Whittier

Happiness depends,
as Nature shows,
Less on exterior things
than most suppose.

William Cowper

Happiness depends upon ourselves.

Aristotle

Man is the artificer of his own happiness.

Henry David Thoreau

Our life is what our thoughts make it.

Marcus Aurelius

Life is what we make it. Always has been. Always will be.

Grandma Moses

Life is 10 percent what you make it and 90 percent how you take it.

Irving Berlin

2

You Made It Another Year: Be Thankful

The fabled Aesop once observed, "Gratitude is the sign of noble souls." A birthday provides the perfect opportunity to nobly give thanks for another year of life.

If we earnestly begin counting our blessings, they add up in a hurry. Henry Van Dyke advised, "Be glad of life because it gives you the chance to love and to work and to play and to look up at the stars." But the list of blessings doesn't stop there. All of us have more good fortune than we recognize.

Today, pause and appreciate some of the things you've been taking for granted. Remember that life, despite its inevitable troubles and inconveniences, is the ultimate gift. Accordingly, it deserves the ultimate gratitude.

A thankful heart is not
only the greatest virtue,
but the parent
of all other virtues.

Cicero

Each day provides its own gifts.

Martial

Gladly accept the gifts of the present hour.

Horace

Count your own blessings
and let your neighbor count his.

James Thurber

Be content with such things as ye have.

Hebrews 13:5

The greatest gifts are those
we give ourselves.

Sophocles

Write it on your heart that every day
is the best day of the year.
Ralph Waldo Emerson

Don't complain about getting old.
Many people don't have that privilege.
Earl Warren

I prefer old age to the alternative.
Maurice Chevalier

I suppose life is a struggle; yet, whenever
I wake up, even with a few hours of sleep,
I feel so glad I'm alive.
Jack Benny

A man is not old
until regrets take
the place of dreams.

John Barrymore

If you love life,
life will love you back.

Artur Rubinstein

Begin at once to live and count each day
as a separate life.

Seneca

A grateful mind is a great mind which
eventually attracts to itself great things.

Plato

Gratitude is the most exquisite form
of courtesy.

Jacques Maritain

Joy is the simplest form of gratitude.

Karl Barth

To know how to grow old is the masterwork
of wisdom, and one of the most difficult
chapters in the great art of living.

Henri Frédéric Amiel

The best is yet to be,
The last of life, for which
the first was made.

Robert Browning

At seventy, I would say the advantage is
that you take life more calmly. You know that
"this too will pass."

Eleanor Roosevelt

Anyone who keeps the ability to see beauty
never grows old.

Kafka

God gave us memories that we might have
roses in December.

James M. Barrie

I don't ask to be young again.
All I want is to go on getting older.

Konrad Adenauer

The best things are nearest.
Do not grasp at the stars, but do life's plain,
common work as it comes, certain that
the daily duties and daily bread
are the sweetest things of life.

Robert Louis Stevenson

As every thread of gold is valuable,
so is every thread of time.

John Mason

Think of all the ills from which you
are exempt.

Joseph Joubert

Having been is the surest kind of being.

Viktor Frankl

Ask not that events happen as they will,
but let your will be that events happen
as they do, and you shall have peace.

Epictetus

He who is contented is rich.

Lao-Tzu

Happy is the man who can count
his sufferings.

Ovid

No life is so hard that you can't make it easier
by the way you take it.

Ellen Glasgow

We are all richer than we think we are.

Michel de Montaigne

Rest and be thankful.

William Wordsworth

Life does not have
to be perfect
to be wonderful.

Annette Funicello

God gave you a gift of
86,400 seconds today.
Have you used one
to say thank you?

William Arthur Ward

3

It's Your Life: Live It!

Father Time keeps a steady pace; we should plan our lives accordingly. As Willa Cather warned, "Life hurries past, too strong to stop, too sweet to lose." Since we can't stop life, or even slow it down for that matter, the only intelligent thing to do is to use it.

If you're chasing a noble dream, congratulations. If you're holding back, be brave and give life a chance. There's precious little to lose and everything to gain. After all, as Jane Ace correctly observed, "We're all cremated equal." So why not live to the fullest in the meantime?

Do not act as if you had a thousand years to live.

Marcus Aurelius

Tomorrow's life is too late. Live today.

Martial

Life is short. Make the most of the present.

Marcus Aurelius

Life is in the living, in the tissue
of every day and hour.

Stephen Leacock

To regret deeply is to live afresh.

Henry David Thoreau

My interest is in the future because I am
going to spend the rest of my life there.

Charles F. Kettering

Time is so precious
that God deals it out
only second by second.

Bishop Fulton J. Sheen

Try to be happy in this very present Moment;
and put not off being so to a Time to come:
as though that Time should be of another
make from this, which is already come
and is ours.

Thomas Fuller

No man has learned anything rightly,
until he knows that everyday is Doomsday.

Ralph Waldo Emerson

A happy life is one that is in accordance
with its own nature.

Seneca

Look well into thyself; there is a source
of strength which will always spring up
if thou will always look there.

Marcus Aurelius

Life is either a daring adventure or nothing.

Helen Keller

The best way to prepare for life
is to begin to live.

Elbert Hubbard

It is not death that a man should fear,
but he should fear never beginning to live.

Marcus Aurelius

The time will come when winter will ask
what you were doing all summer.

Henry Clay

Every man's life lies within the present, for the past is spent and the future is uncertain.

Marcus Aurelius

When life kicks you, let it kick you forward.

E. Stanley Jones

Use the best vase today, for tomorrow it may, perchance, be broken.

The Talmud

Do noble things, do not dream them all day long.

Charles Kingsley

Don't believe there's plenty
of time for everything.
There isn't.

Lillian Hellman

The Bird of Time has but a little way
to flutter — and the bird is on the wing.

Omar Khayyám

Life has got to be lived.
That's all there is to it.

Eleanor Roosevelt

Time is really the only capital that any
human being has and the only thing
he can't afford to lose.

Thomas Edison

Tomorrow's life is too late. Live today.

Martial

The passing minute is every man's
equal possession.

Marcus Aurelius

Life is too short
to be small.

Benjamin Disraeli

Hope for the best. Expect the worst.
Life is a play. We're unrehearsed.

Mel Brooks

Fear not that thy life shall come to an end,
but rather fear that it shall never have
a beginning.

John Henry Cardinal Newman

Time and tide wait for no man.

Sir Walter Scott

Here's a new day. O pendulum move slowly!

Harold Munro

Do not walk through time without leaving
worthy evidence of your passage.

Pope John XXIII

Live your life and forget your age.

Frank Bering

The right time is any time that one is still
so lucky as to have ... Live!

Henry James

No man loves life like he who is growing old.

Sophocles

Life is too good to waste a day.
It's up to you to make it sweet.

Sadie Delany

Always hold fast to the present.
Every situation, indeed every moment, is of
infinite value, for it is the representative
of a whole eternity.

Goethe

May you live all the days of your life.

Jonathan Swift

4

It's Your Party:
Invite Your Friends

Birthdays and solitude don't mix. So even if you're a hermit for the other 364 days of the year, round up your pals for today's celebration.

Ralph Waldo Emerson wrote, "A friend may well be reckoned a masterpiece of nature." Had he been in a birthday mood, Emerson might have added that friendships are the icing on the cake of life. Today, on this special day, your cake deserves lots of icing.

What is a friend?
A single soul dwelling
in two bodies.

Aristotle

There is nothing on this earth more
  to be prized than true friendship.

St. Thomas Aquinas

A friend is one who makes me do my best.

Oswald Chambers

The wise man seeks a friend with qualities
  he himself lacks.

Jeremy Taylor

A sympathetic friend can be quite as dear
  as a brother.

Homer

Friendship flourishes at the fountain
of forgiveness.

William Arthur Ward

We have no more right to consume
happiness without producing it than
to consume wealth without producing it.

George Bernard Shaw

A true friend is the most precious
of all possessions and the one we take
the least thought about acquiring.

La Rochefoucauld

Where there are friends, there is wealth.

Latin Proverb

A friend is a present
you give yourself.

Robert Louis Stevenson

Shared joys make a friend,
      not shared sufferings.

Goethe

The only way to have a friend is to be one.

Ralph Waldo Emerson

The comfort of having a friend may be taken
away, but not that of having had one.

Seneca

'Tis better to be alone than in bad company.

George Washington

Cheerful company shortens the miles.

German Proverb

Life is partly what we make it and partly
what is made by the friends we choose.

Chinese Proverb

True happiness consists not in the multitude
of friends, but in the worth and choice.

Ben Johnson

The fingers of God touch your life
when you touch a friend.

Mary Dawn Hughes

Tell me with whom thou art found and
I will tell thee who thou art.

Goethe

The language of friendship is not words, but meanings.

Henry David Thoreau

.

It is more shameful to distrust our friends
than to be deceived by them.

La Rochefoucauld

Thanks cost nothing.

Southern Saying

The ornaments of our house are the friends
who frequent it.

Ralph Waldo Emerson

Friendships form among people
who strengthen one another.

Franklin Owen

Man's best support is a very dear friend.

Cicero

5

Life Is Opportunity: Seize It

Samuel Johnson correctly observed, "Life, like every other blessing, derives its value from its use alone." How do we best use the gift of life? By taking advantage of the opportunities that surround us each day.

For the human race, the operative tense is the future tense. The importance of the future is obvious: Everything that happens from now on takes place there.

If today is your birthday, be forewarned: This is the first day of the rest of your year. So why not consider your options? If you mistakenly believe that your options are few, think again. Life is like a supermarket with opportunities bulging from every aisle. But it's your job to fill the cart.

It is not how many years we live, but what we do with them.

Evangeline Booth

Life is available
to anyone no matter
what age. All you have
to do is grab it.

Art Carney

Take a chance. All life is a chance.

Dale Carnegie

Life shrinks or expands in proportion
to one's courage.

Anaïs Nin

Learn what you are and be such.

Pindar

The tragedy of life is not so much what men
suffer, but what they miss.

Thomas Carlyle

Make your life a mission —
not an intermission.

Arnold Glasgow

As soon as you trust yourself,
you will know how to live.

Goethe

Life is doing things, not making things.

Aristotle

There's an old saying that life begins at 40.
That's silly. Life begins every morning
when you wake up.

George Burns

Life is painting a picture, not doing a sum.

Oliver Wendell Holmes, Jr.

A wise man will make more opportunities
than he finds.

Francis Bacon

All life is an experiment.
The more experiments you make, the better.

Ralph Waldo Emerson

Do you love life? Then do not squander
time, for that's the stuff life is made of.

Ben Franklin

Live from miracle to miracle.

Artur Rubinstein

He who desires, but acts not,
breeds pestilence.

William Blake

Plunge boldly into the thick of life!

Goethe

The man who insists upon seeing
with perfect clearness before he decides,
never decides.

Henri Frédéric Amiel

The best way to make
your dreams come true
is to wake up.

Paul Valéry

One today is worth two tomorrows.

Ben Franklin

This time, like all times, is a very good one,
if we only know what to do with it.

Ralph Waldo Emerson

Our main business is not to see what lies
dimly at a distance, but to do what lies
clearly at hand.

Thomas Carlyle

Life is no brief candle to me. It is a sort of
splendid torch which I have got hold of for
the moment, and I want to make it burn as
brightly as possible before handing it on
to future generations.

George Bernard Shaw

Great minds have purposes,
others have wishes.

Washington Irving

It is *now* and in *this world* that we must live.

André Gide

Dying seems less sad than having lived
too little.

Gloria Steinem

The great use of life is to spend it
for something that will outlast it.

William James

Life is a series of collisions with the future;
it is not a sum of what we have been
but what we yearn to be.

José Ortega y Gasset

Things are only worth
what you make them worth.

Moliére

The real fear is not death — it is the fear
of wasting life.

Jackie Gleason

Do something worth remembering.

Elvis Presley

Find the journey's end in every step.

Ralph Waldo Emerson

6

Behave Yourself: It's More Fun

When you were young, you probably heard the words "behave yourself" a thousand times. All the while, you thought that adults were trying to ruin your fun. By now you may have learned the sobering truth: In the long run, it's actually more fun to behave.

Socrates noted, "Living well and beautifully and justly are all the same thing." Noted actress Loretta Young echoed those words when she advised, "Listen to your conscience, and it will serve you as no other friend you'll ever know."

Birthdays, along with all the other days, are happiest when we behave ourselves. After all, life is a party, so why spoil it?

A man cannot be comfortable
without his own approval.

Mark Twain

Rule your desires lest your desires rule you.

Publilius Syrus

Would you live with ease, do what you ought,
and not what you please.

Ben Franklin

A man, after he has brushed off the dust and
chips of his life, will have left only the hard,
clean question: Was it good or was it evil?
Have I done well — or ill?

John Steinbeck

The saints are sinners
who keep on going.

Robert Louis Stevenson

Character is simply habit long continued.
Plutarch

Character is power.
Booker T. Washington

If you do evil, expect to suffer evil.
Spanish Proverb

A man's character is his fate.
Heraclitus

Only the just man enjoys peace of mind.
Epictetus

If rascals knew the advantages of virtue, they would become honest.

Ben Franklin

Don't compromise
yourself. You're
all you've got.

Janis Joplin

When we do the best we can, we never
know what miracles await.

Helen Keller

People should think less about what they
ought to do, and more about what they ought
to be. If only their living were good,
their work would shine forth brightly.

Meister Eckhart

Live not as if you had ten thousand years
before you. Necessity is upon you. While you
live, while you may, become good.

Marcus Aurelius

We are not punished for our sins,
but by them.

Elbert Hubbard

Act well at the moment, and you have
performed a good action for all eternity.

Johann K. Lavater

Rudeness is the weak man's imitation
of strength.

Eric Hoffer

We are happier in many ways when we are
old than when we were young.
The young sow wild oats.
The old grow sage.

Winston Churchill

Make us happy and you make us good.

Robert Browning

T
rue happiness is not attained through
self-gratification but through fidelity
to a worthy cause.

Helen Keller

D
on't mistake pleasure for happiness.

Josh Billings

B
e virtuous and you'll be happy? Nonsense!
Be happy and you'll begin to be virtuous.

James Gould Cozzens

Middle age is when you're faced with
two temptations, and you choose the one
that gets you home by nine o'clock.

Ronald Reagan

Enough is as good as a feast.

John Heywood

Most people who fly from temptation
usually leave a forwarding address.

Anonymous

It is easier to stay out than to get out.

Mark Twain

It is one thing
to be tempted,
another thing to fall.

William Shakespeare

I can resist everything
except temptation.

Oscar Wilde

7

Never Stop Growing Up

At age 75, arthritis made it difficult for Grandma Moses to enjoy her favorite hobby, embroidery. So she took up painting. Before her death at age 101, she had become a beloved American artist and a cultural treasure. When asked about her work, she responded, "Painting is not important. The important thing is keeping busy."

As another birthday rolls around, consider the example of Grandma Moses. Long after her allotted three score and ten, she discovered a new passion that enriched her life and the lives of others. All because she taught herself a new skill.

Someone once said, "It's never too late to have a happy childhood." Grandma Moses proved that it's never too late to learn, and it's never too late to enjoy your education.

Man's main task in life is giving birth
to himself.

Erich Fromm

The art of living lies less in eliminating
our troubles than in growing with them.

Bernard Baruch

All growth is a leap in the dark.

Henry Miller

Be not afraid of growing slowly, be afraid
only of standing still.

Chinese Proverb

The days in my life that stand out most
vividly are the days I've learned something.
Learning is so exciting I get goose bumps.

Lucille Ball

Growth is the only evidence of life.

John Henry Cardinal Newman

Happiness to me means constant growth.

Eddie Albert

You grow up the day you have
your first real laugh at yourself.

Ethel Barrymore

The education of a man is completed only
when he dies.

Robert E. Lee

I grow old ever learning many things.

Solon

You don't grow old. When you cease to grow,
you *are* old.

Charles Judson Herrick

In youth we learn. In age we understand.

Marie Ebner-Eschenbach

When you're green
you're growing,
when you're ripe
you rot.

Ray Kroc

The wish to progress is the largest part
of progress.

Seneca

As long as you live, keep learning
how to live.

Seneca

I am still learning.

Michelangelo's Motto

A man, though wise, should never be
ashamed of learning more.

Sophocles

We are constantly becoming what eventually
we are going to be.

Samuel Johnson

No man need stay the way he is.

Harry Emerson Fosdick

Always be in a state of becoming.

Walt Disney

The best song of your life may be
just around the corner.

Keith Richards

Adapt or perish, now as ever,
    is nature's inexorable imperative.

H. G. Wells

If you do what you've always done,
    you'll get what you always got.

Anonymous

Nothing endures but change.

Heraclitus

Only in growth, reform, and change,
paradoxically enough, is true security found.

Anne Morrow Lindbergh

Don't be afraid to take a big step if one
is indicated. You can't cross a chasm
in two small jumps.

David Lloyd George

The shell must break before the bird can fly.

Alfred, Lord Tennyson

If I had my life to live over, I'd make
the same mistakes, only sooner.

Tallulah Bankhead

On the human chessboard,
all moves are possible.

Miriam Schiff

Men of seventy or eighty are often more
youthful than the young. Youth has to do
with spirit, not age.

Henry Miller

We must not stay as we are, doing always
what was done last time, or we shall stick
in the mud.

George Bernard Shaw

The secret of happiness is this:
Let your interests be as wide as possible, and
let your reactions to the things and persons
that interest you be as far as possible friendly
rather than hostile.

Bertrand Russell

The great law of culture is: Let each become
all that he was capable of being; expand,
if possible, to his full growth.

Thomas Carlyle

What we are
is God's gift to us.
What we become
is our gift to God.

Eleanor Powell

Winter is on my head, but eternal spring is in my heart.

Victor Hugo

I like dreams of the future better than
the history of the past.

Thomas Jefferson

Destiny is not a matter of chance,
it is a matter of choice.

William Jennings Bryan

We are all functioning at a small fraction
of our capacity. Consequently, the actualizing
of our potential can become the most exciting
adventure of our lifetime.

Herbert Otto

Life is like a ten-speed bike. Most of us have
gears we never use.

Charles Schulz

Experience is only half of experience.

Goethe

All that I know I learned after thirty.

Georges Clemenceau

The compensation of growing old
was simply this: that the passions remain as
strong as ever, but one has gained — at last! —
the power which adds the supreme flavor
to existence, the power of taking hold
of experience, of turning it round,
slowly, in the light.

Virginia Woolf

The man of true greatness never loses
his child's heart.

Mencius

Youth is the time for adventures of the body,
but age for the triumphs of his mind.

Logan Pearsall Smith

Success consists in the climb.

Elbert Hubbard

A man should never stop learning,
even on his last day.

Maimonides

It is better to wear out than to rust.

Richard Cumberland

Anyone who stops learning is old,
whether at twenty or eighty.

Henry Ford

I am long on ideas but short on time.
I expect to live to be only about a hundred.

Thomas Edison

Whatever you can do or dream you can, begin it. Boldness has genius, power and magic in it.

Goethe

8

Stay Young at Heart

Robert Louis Stevenson wrote, "Childhood must pass away, and then youth, as surely as age approaches. The true wisdom is to be always seasonable, and to change with a good grace in changing circumstances."

How do we change with good grace? By maintaining a childlike sense of joy and wonder. The world can be a happy, entertaining place, especially for a child. To a young boy or girl, every experience is new, breathtaking, even humorous. Grown-ups are advised to take notice. Whether we're enjoying the spring, summer, fall or winter of life, a youthful heart is always in season.

The mind is like a clock that is constantly running down. It has to be wound up daily with good thoughts.

Bishop Fulton J. Sheen

You can't turn back the clock.
But you can wind it up again.

Bonnie Prudden

Thou canst begin a new life! See but things afresh as thou used to see them;
for in this consists the new life.

Marcus Aurelius

You're never too old to become younger.

Mae West

The significant tense for human beings is the future tense.

Rollo May

I don't like looking back. I'm looking ahead to the next show. It's how I keep young.

Jack Benny

It is important to stay close enough to the
pulse of life to feel its rhythm, to be
comforted by its steadiness, to know that
life is vital, and one's own minute living
a torn fragment of the larger cloth.

Marjorie Kinnan Rawlings

Follow your desire as long as you live;
do not lessen the time of following desire,
for the wasting of time is an abomination
to the spirit.

Ptahhotep

Youth is, after all, just a moment, but it is
the moment, the spark you can always carry
in your heart.

Raisa Gorbachev

No wise man ever wished to be younger.

Jonathan Swift

There is one thing which gives radiance
to everything. It is the idea of something
around the corner.

G. K. Chesterton

We are always the same age inside.

Gertrude Stein

To remain young, one must change.

Alexander Chase

Never run out of goals.

Earl Nightingale

I don't think you should quit working, ever.
If you do have to retire, find something else
to do. You've got to keep your mind busy or
you'll spend too much time dwelling
on unpleasant things.

Milton Berle

The secret of a long life is double careers.
One to about age 60, then another
for the next 30 years.

David Ogilvy

You must keep busy. Continue working
if you can, or develop an interest that you
can pursue as though it were a livelihood.
Activity is the only antidote.

B. F. Skinner

Life is like a bicycle: You don't fall off
unless you stop pedaling.

Claude Pepper

Woe to the man whose heart has not learned
while young to hope, to live, to love —
and to put its trust in life!

Joseph Conrad

There are very few things you can do to defy
the aging process. Keeping your hopes alive
is definitely one of them.

Dr. Stanley H. Cath

Most people say that as you get old,
you have to give up things. I think you get old
because you give up things.

Theodore Francis Green

If you are losing your leisure, look out!
You are losing your soul.

Logan Pearsall Smith

Happy is the man who gains sagacity
in youth, but thrice happy is he who retains
the fervour of youth.

Dagobert Runes

He who is of a calm and happy nature
will hardly feel the pressure of age.

Plato

There is no cosmetic like happiness.

Lady Marguerite Blessington

Age is a matter of feeling, not of years.

George William Curtis

Old people don't get tired — it's only the young who tire. Confusion exhausts them. I've got more energy now than when I was younger because I know exactly what I want to do.

George Balanchine

Age is only a number. Experience achieves more with less energy and time.

Bernard Baruch

Age is bothersome only when you stop to coddle it.

Maurice Chevalier

It's not how old you are, but how you are old.

Marie Dressler

Age is a case of mind over matter.
If you don't mind, it doesn't matter.

Jack Benny

For the unlearned, old age is winter;
for the learned, it is the harvest.

Hasidic Saying

In the midst of winter, I finally learned that
there was in me an invincible summer.

Albert Camus

Age is not important unless you're a cheese.

Helen Hayes

For what has been —
thanks.
For what shall be — yes.

Dag Hammarskjöld

9

Share Your Gifts

The greatest gifts are shared gifts. Lord Byron observed, "All who would win joy must share it. Happiness was born a twin." These words are wonderful advice for birthdays and non-birthdays alike. Had Lord Byron been a gambling man, he would have understood this simple truth: Happiness, though sometimes a roll of the dice, is always double or nothing.

Be kind, for everyone
you meet is fighting
a hard battle.

Philo

Be big enough to serve other people.

Claude Pepper

A life isn't significant except for its impact on other lives.

Jackie Robinson

Success has nothing to do with what you gain in life or accomplish for yourself. It's what you do for others.

Danny Thomas

The older you get, the more you realize that kindness is synonymous with happiness.

Lionel Barrymore

He does good to himself who does good to his friend.

Erasmus

Above all things have fervent charity
among yourselves. For charity shall cover
a multitude of sins.

I Peter 4:8

The rich man is not one who is in possession
of much, but one who gives much.

St. John Chrysostom

And now abideth faith, hope, and charity,
these three; but the greatest of these
is charity.

I Corinthians 13:13

Look to be treated by others
as you have treated others.

Publilius Syrus

You have to help your friends,
or you won't have any.

Russell B. Long

Unshared joy is an unlighted candle.

Spanish Proverb

Get not your friends by bare compliments,
but by giving them sensible tokens of love.

Socrates

We cannot live only for ourselves.
A thousand fibers connect us
with our fellow man.

Herman Melville

Our duty is to be useful, not according
to our desires, but according to our powers.

Henri Frédéric Amiel

Help thy brother's boat across, and lo!
Thine own has reached the shore.

Hindu Proverb

If I can stop one heart from breaking,
     I shall not live in vain.

Emily Dickinson

The best way to cheer yourself up
     is to try to cheer somebody else up.

Mark Twain

Think as little as possible about yourself and
     as much as possible about other people.

Eleanor Roosevelt

Every charitable act is a stepping stone
     toward heaven.

Henry Ward Beecher

Be a friend to thyself,
     and others will be so too.

Thomas Fuller

No person was ever honored for what
he received. Honor has been the reward
for what he gave.

Calvin Coolidge

It is more blessed to give than to receive.

Acts 20:35

Charity makes no decrease in property.

Arabian Proverb

A man wrapped up in himself makes
a very small package.

Ben Franklin

The best portion of a good man's life:
his little, nameless, unremembered acts
of kindness and of love.

William Wordsworth

You cannot do a kindness too soon because
you never know how soon it will be too late.

Ralph Waldo Emerson

Men of the noblest dispositions think
themselves happiest when others share
their happiness with them.

Jeremy Taylor

An act of goodness is of itself
an act of happiness.

Maurice Maeterlinck

To live is not to live for one's self alone;
let us help one another.

Menander

No act of kindness, no matter how small,
is ever wasted.

Aesop

A loving person lives in a loving world.
A hostile person lives in a hostile world.
Everyone you meet is your mirror.

Ken Keyes, Jr.

He whose face gives no light shall never
be a star.

William Blake

What do we live for, if it is not to make life
less difficult for each other?

George Eliot

Become genuinely interested
in other people.

Dale Carnegie

Make yourself necessary to somebody.

Ralph Waldo Emerson

The greatest good you can do for another
is not just to share your riches but
to reveal to him his own.

Benjamin Disraeli

Kind words can be short and easy to speak,
but their echoes are truly endless.

Mother Teresa

Keep your fears to yourself, but share your courage.

Robert Louis Stevenson

The heart that loves is always young.

Greek Proverb

10

You're Another Year Better: Celebrate!

An English proverb states, "The older the fiddle, the sweeter the tune." It follows that your fiddle is another year better and your tune is another year sweeter. That calls for a celebration! Happy Birthday, and may you enjoy many more.

Men are like wine. Some turn to vinegar, but the best improve with age.

Thomas Henry Huxley

Where we stand is not as important
as the direction in which we are moving.
Oliver Wendell Holmes, Jr.

People wish to be settled; but it is only as far
as they are unsettled that there is
any hope for them.
Ralph Waldo Emerson

Arriving at one goal is the starting point
of another.
John Dewey

To be interested in the changing seasons
is a happier state of mind than to be
hopelessly in love with spring.
George Santayana

Change is the only evidence of life.
Evelyn Waugh

Experience teaches.

Tacitus

Experience is not what happens to you; it is what you do with what happens to you.

Aldous Huxley

Life is a series of lessons that must be lived to be understood.

Ralph Waldo Emerson

A proverb is no proverb to you until life has illustrated it.

John Keats

It's what you learn after you know it all that counts.

Harry Truman

Almost all absurdity of conduct arises from
the imitation of those we cannot resemble.

Samuel Johnson

Strengthen yourself with contentment
for it is an impregnable fortress.

Epictetus

My recipe for life is not being afraid
of myself.

Eartha Kitt

Resolve to be thyself;
and know that he who finds himself,
loses his misery.

Matthew Arnold

Assume responsibility for the quality of your own life.

Norman Cousins

One faces the future with one's past.

Pearl Buck

The evening of a well-spent life brings
its lamp with it.

Joseph Joubert

The young man knows the rules,
but the old man knows the exceptions.

Oliver Wendell Holmes

Life is a language in which certain truths
are conveyed to us; if we could learn them
in some other way, we should not live.

Schopenhauer

Nobody ever drew up his plans for life
so well but what the facts and the years of
experience always introduce
some modification.

Terence

Make it a rule of life never to regret and never to look back. Regret is an appalling waste of energy; you can't build on it; it's only good for wallowing in.

Katherine Mansfield

Keep company with those who may make you better.

English Saying

The spiritual eyesight improves as the physical eyesight declines.

Plato

Ask the God who made you to keep remaking you.

Norman Vincent Peale

Memory is the mother of all wisdom.

Aeschylus

The hours of a wise man are lengthened
by his ideas.

Joseph Addison

Long years must pass before the truths
we have made for ourselves become
our very flesh.

Paul Valéry

How unhappy is he
who cannot forgive himself.

Publilius Syrus

Nothing in life is to be feared.
It is only to be understood.

Marie Curie

Life can only be understood backwards,
but must be lived forward.

Søren Kierkegaard

The years teach much which the days
never know.

Ralph Waldo Emerson

Let us respect gray hairs, especially our own.

J. P. Senn

To me, old age is always fifteen years older
than I am.

Bernard Baruch

Old age is like everything else.
To make a success of it,
you've got to start young.

Fred Astaire

The little present must not be allowed
to wholly elbow the great past out of view.

Andrew Lang

While I would not have missed yesterday,
I have no desire to go back and live it over.
For me, there is only the great today and
the promise of tomorrow.

Mary Pickford

The future is not ominous, but a promise.
It surrounds the present like a halo.

John Dewey

Fear not for the future, weep not for the past.

Percy Bysshe Shelley

The past is history. Make the present good,
and the past will take care of itself.

Knute Rockne

Do not take life
too seriously.
You'll never
get out of it alive.

Elbert Hubbard

I am what I am!
That's a great thing to be!
If I say so myself,
HAPPY BIRTHDAY TO ME!

Dr. Seuss

Sources

Sources

Jane Ace 49
Joseph Addison 150
Konrad Adenauer 43
Aeschylus 29, 150
Aesop 35, 137
Eddie Albert 103
Henri Frédéric Amiel 42, 82, 133
St. Thomas Aquinas 65
Aristotle 33, 64, 80
Matthew Arnold 146
Fred Astaire 151
Jane Austen 16
Francis Bacon 81
George Balanchine 126
Lucille Ball 103
Tallulah Bankhead 109
James M. Barrie 43
Ethel Barrymore 103
John Barrymore 39
Lionel Barrymore 131
Karl Barth 41
Bernard Baruch 28, 102, 126, 151
Charles Baudelaire 24
Henry Ward Beecher 134
Ludwig van Beethoven 22
Jack Benny 38, 119, 127
Frank Bering 60
Milton Berle 122
Irving Berlin 34
Josh Billings 97
William Blake 82, 137
Lady Marguerite Blessington 125
Evangeline Booth 76
Mel Brooks 59
Robert Browning 42, 96
William Jennings Bryan 113
Pearl Buck 148
George Burns 81
Lord Byron 129
Albert Camus 127
Thomas Carlyle 79, 85, 110
Dale Carnegie 22, 78, 138

Art Carney 77
Dr. Stanley H. Cath 123
Willa Cather 49
Miguel de Cervantes 22
Oswald Chambers 65
Alexander Chase 121
G. K. Chesterton 121
Maurice Chevalier 38, 126
St. John Chrysostom 132
Winston Churchill 31, 96
Cicero 36, 74
Henry Clay 54
Georges Clemenceau 114
Joseph Conrad 123
Calvin Coolidge 135
Norman Cousins 147
William Cowper 32
James Gould Cozzens 97
Richard Cumberland 115
Marie Curie 150
George William Curtis 126
Sadie Delany 61
John Dewey 143, 152
Emily Dickinson 134
Walt Disney 17, 107
Benjamin Disraeli 58, 138
Dorothy Dix 30
Marie Dressler 126
Marie Ebner-Eschenbach 104
Thomas Edison 57, 115
George Eliot 138
Ralph Waldo Emerson 21, 38, 53, 63, 68, 73, 81, 88, 136, 138, 143, 144, 151
Epictetus 26, 45, 92, 146
Erasmus 131
Euripides 18
William Feather 17
Harry Emerson Fosdick 107
Henry Ford 115
Viktor Frankl 45
Ben Franklin 81, 84, 90, 93, 135
Erich Fromm 102
Thomas Fuller 134
Annette Funicello 47

Sources

About Wisdom Books

Wisdom Books chronicle memorable quotations in an easy-to-read style. Written by Criswell Freeman, this series provides inspiring, thoughtful and humorous messages from entertainers, athletes, scientists, politicians, clerics, writers and renegades. Each title focuses on a particular region or area of special interest.

Combining his passion for quotations with extensive training in psychology, Dr. Freeman revisits timeless themes such as perseverance, courage, love, forgiveness and faith.

"Quotations help us remember the simple yet profound truths that give life perspective and meaning," notes Freeman. "When it comes to life's most important lessons, we can all use gentle reminders."

About the Author

Criswell Freeman is a Doctor of Clinical Psychology living in Nashville, Tennessee. He is the author of *When Life Throws You a Curveball, Hit It* and *The Wisdom Series* from WALNUT GROVE PRESS.

The Wisdom Series
by Dr. Criswell Freeman

Regional Titles

Wisdom Made in America	ISBN 1-887655-07-7
The Book of Southern Wisdom	ISBN 0-9640955-3-X
The Wisdom of the Midwest	ISBN 1-887655-17-4
The Wisdom of the West	ISBN 1-887655-31-X
The Book of Texas Wisdom	ISBN 0-9640955-8-0
The Book of Florida Wisdom	ISBN 0-9640955-9-9
The Book of California Wisdom	ISBN 1-887655-14-X
The Book of New York Wisdom	ISBN 1-887655-16-6
The Book of New England Wisdom	ISBN 1-887655-15-8

Sports Titles

The Golfer's Book of Wisdom	ISBN 0-9640955-6-4
The Putter Principle	ISBN 1-887655-39-5
The Golfer's Guide to Life	ISBN 1-887655-38-7
The Wisdom of Southern Football	ISBN 0-9640955-7-2
The Book of Stock Car Wisdom	ISBN 1-887655-12-3
The Wisdom of Old-Time Baseball	ISBN 1-887655-08-5
The Book of Football Wisdom	ISBN 1-887655-18-2
The Book of Basketball Wisdom	ISBN 1-887655-32-8
The Fisherman's Guide to Life	ISBN 1-887655-30-1

Special Interest Titles

The Book of Country Music Wisdom	ISBN 0-9640955-1-3
The Wisdom of Old-Time Television	ISBN 1-887655-64-6
The Wisdom of the Heart	ISBN 1-887655-34-4
The Guide to Better Birthdays	ISBN 1-887655-35-2
The Gardener's Guide to Life	ISBN 1-887655-40-9
Minutes from the Great Women's Coffee Club (by Angela Beasley)	ISBN 1-887655-33-6

Wisdom Books are available through booksellers everywhere.
For information about a retailer near you, call 1-800-256-8584.